To You
Cent to .
You help
You Know!

[signature]

DIVINE
Healings

DIVINE
Healings

Yolanda Ceasar

iUniverse, Inc.
Bloomington

Divine Healings

iUniverse books may be ordered through booksellers or by contacting:

iUniverse
1663 Liberty Drive
Bloomington, IN 47403
www.iuniverse.com
1-800-Authors (1-800-288-4677)

ISBN: 978-1-4759-7613-7 (sc)
ISBN: 978-1-4759-7614-4 (ebk)

Printed in the United States of America

iUniverse rev. date: 02/21/2013

This book is Dedicated to

My sisters, Gail Ceasar, Nicole Anthony, my brother, Dwight, my children, Bianca and Brandon, Mother, Victoria, Pastor and Lady Knotts, Apostle Virginia West and Elder West; my children's father Andre Crews who I am partnered with in C&C Cleaning Solutions and bestfriend Tashanna Bauldwin-Lindsay Prince Charles Enterprise.

Contents

PREFACE

It is so important for us to be honest with ourselves, others, and God in reference to where we are. How can we be helped if we don't admit to who we are, how we are feeling, and where we are? God's love and mercy are for our freedom. It is not his desire that his children suffer in bondage. Only God can bring true deliverance and healing. Only we can accept it. If we can easily accept the doctor's report or someone telling us we are sick, why can't we accept someone telling us we are healed?

I suffered from depression for five years. I don't quite remember how I became depressed. The pressures of ministry and being faithful to people caused me to become resentful and angry. It was like I saw a light at the end of the tunnel, but I couldn't get my mind or body to move in that direction. There were times when I wanted to die, but I didn't want to kill myself (because I would surely go to hell). I didn't want anyone to kill me because I was afraid of the pain! My God, what a demon I fought!

I am being honest and transparent so that no one feels I did not need a healer. Yes, it sounds crazy, but I was there in that place ministering, laying hands on the sick, and watching them recover. I was sick with depression and had two children. Instead of dying physically, I died to the pleasures of life. Anger grew in my heart. I am passionate about my current relationship with God because of where I've been with him. If it wasn't for God, I would not be where I am now.

I am well acquainted with grief, hopelessness, and loneliness. The devil always draws your attention to what you are lacking rather than to what you have. My desires for what I wanted were so strong and so intense that the fire and passion quickly burned out. I had to keep living because of my children.

Depression is real. It is a spirit. Christians are subject to this spirit when we become disobedient and walk outside the will of God. Our inability to handle the pressures of life effectively will also cause us to walk with depression. God gives us hope. He shows us through the life of Ezekiel that we are not bound by depression if we have belief in him. He shows us through the life of Jeremiah that we can still focus and function through it all. He shows us how he can deliver us through obedience with the life of Jonah. God also shows us that there is a peak and that the breaking point can lead to grace through Jesus's cry: "Why hast thou forsaken me?"

Jesus shows us through sensitivity and compassion that we who are stronger should bear the infirmities of the weaker (Romans 15:1). However, if we allow ourselves to get lost in our lack, we cannot see the need or lack in our brothers' or sisters' lives. I cannot love my brethren if I have no love for myself. It is through our relationship with God and those close to us that depression is truly broken. If we obey Philippians 4:7, depression should never violate our lives.

"We then that are strong ought to bear the infirmities of the weak, and not to please ourselves" (Romans 15:1).

"Finally, brethren, whatsoever things are true, whatsoever things are honest, whatsoever things are just, whatsoever things are pure, whatsoever things are lovely, whatsoever things are of good report; if there be any virtue, and if there be any praise, think on these things. Those things, which ye have both learned, and received, and heard, and seen in me, do: and the God of peace shall be with you" (Philippians 4:8–9).

I had to begin to think positive things and believe my situation could change. I had to believe that God loved me enough to want me to have a better life. This change had to begin in my mind. The seed of positive thinking was planted in my mind from hearing the words preached by my pastor.

The scriptures tell us that faith comes from hearing (Romans 10:17). The more we hear a certain word, the more likely we are to believe the word that is being said. This can be negative or positive.

I was five foot six and 150 pounds, with wider hips than my slender aunts and female cousins. They constantly told me I was fat—and that I would become fatter. Coupled with my insecurities, I finally believed I was fat. My appetite and behavior began to simulate an obese person's. Obsessive binge eating, fatigue from poor dieting, and a lack of activity fueled the thoughts that I was fat.

One day, I noticed I was more than fifty pounds overweight. I didn't believe I could be beautiful because of the negative words and comments I heard daily about my weight. The excess weight burned away my confidence. Although I desperately wanted to marry, I pushed away good men because of my low self-esteem and insecurity. This was no way to live my life.

Instead of using the Holy Spirit as the comforter he is, food was my comfort. I will go into great details in my next book, *Destroying Beauty*, which deals with eating disorders and identity problems. Binge eating, overeating, or indulging in unhealthy pleasurable foods are weapons of the enemy. These weapons are used to destroy the one thing that is most precious to God: the soul! I share this because I have experienced true deliverance in my body from obesity and my soul from depression. Also his grace has allowed me to heal from being a contrite, wounded spirit. Recovery is a long, tough road. If we follow Jesus's instruction and example, we too can live victorious lives!

INTRODUCTION

I would like to thank Rick Pino; his song "Zerubbabel" inspired and reminded me that when I enter the presence of God, my innocence is restored.

The first thing that must happen before true deliverance can take place is the acknowledgment that there is an issue that is causing the present pain. This present pain can be symptoms of an illness, disease, or condition that you are experiencing in your spirit, body, or soul. The pain is real physically, emotionally, or spiritually—and it is what you say it is. We have to remember that in all physical, mental, or spiritual adversity, we are never alone.

God is our creator; he is the great I Am, Alpha and Omega, the beginning and end (Revelation 1:11). He is there when we feel his presence and when we don't. His arms are not too short to save us, and his power is not too weak to heal us (Isaiah 59:1). He is desperate to show his might and strength to us (2 Chronicles 16:9). He is the author and finisher of our faith (Hebrews 12:2). He is Lord.

"For the eyes of the LORD run to and fro throughout the whole earth, to shew himself strong in the behalf of them whose heart is perfect toward him" (2 Chronicles 16:9).

"Behold, the Lord's hand is not shortened, that it cannot save; neither his ear heavy, that it cannot hear" (Isaiah 59:1).

"Looking unto Jesus the author and finisher of our faith; who for the joy that was set before him endured the cross, despising the shame, and is set down at the right hand of the throne of God" (Hebrews 12:2).

"I am Alpha and Omega, the beginning and the ending, saith the Lord, which is, and which was, and which is to come, the Almighty" (Revelation 1:8).

CHAPTER 1
Pain

Pain is an unpleasant sensation occurring in varying degrees of severity as a consequence of injury, disease, or emotional disorder. Pain causes suffering and distress. All pain that is experienced—whether emotional, physical, or spiritual—is real to the individual experiencing it. Ultimately, if not dealt with or treated, it will cause death.

Pain can be taken as good or bad. It can be taken as bitter or sweet, as poison or a cure, or as death or life. Pain is never alone, and it cannot originate alone. It is a symptom that follows an injury, disease, or condition.

Pain is only as big as its originator. The severity of the pain is determined by its location, duration, and purpose. Pain can be treated, but it can only be cured by eradicating the source of the pain. In order to eradicate, destroy, or cast down the source of pain, we must first acknowledge that there is pain. Second, we must accept that there is a cause for the pain. Third, we must seek help or understanding of where the pain is coming from—and sometimes why we are experiencing the pain. When looking at pain as a symptom of bigger issues, it helps to understand a little pathology and neurology of pain perception. Pain or feelings of pain can be experienced when our touch sensation is overstimulated. There are many types of receptors in the body. The receptors for pain are called nociceptors. Neurons take the signals up to the brain from the nociceptors.

When we touch something that causes an unpleasant sensation, it is received by the nociceptors. From there, it is transferred to neurons that carry the signal to the brain. The brain will interpret the pain, its severity, and where it originated. Maybe that's what happened to man in the Garden of Eden. Not only did he touch the forbidden tree, he ate of the forbidden fruit. Thus, generations of pain originated in our bellies (or spirit), and Adam and Eve died!

There are many symptoms to different diseases, but pain seems to be a common factor. Too much of anything will always result in pain. With a common cold, people typically experience minor pain. This pain is caused by a virus that produces a variety of symptoms. However, the virus that causes the common cold doesn't cause excruciating pain. However, if you have a little headache from the common cold, and it triggers a bigger headache or a migraine, you will be forced to treat the headache with medicine, rest, or going to a doctor. All pain produces the same results. The result is seeking treatment.

We often deny ourselves treatment because we decide the pain is not relevant at the time. If we ignore the pain, it might resolve itself on its own. Let's look at emotional pain. Emotional pain is felt in our emotions. When we are sad, we cry. When we are angry, we reveal the anger in our actions or by withdraw.

If a person in emotional pain offends you by not speaking to you or says something you don't like, is it really about you? Is the pain originating inside? The person might not seek counsel because they are not aware that their pain is causing someone else's pain. The pain is not relevant until there has been damage to—or complete severance of—the relationship. It is the same with physical pain. How often do people not seek treatment for physical pain until there is physical damage or the pain is unbearable?

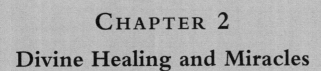

Chapter 2

Divine Healing and Miracles

We can define healing as the natural process by which the body repairs itself! When we look at healing, we can actually look at healing on three dimensions. The dimensions are man, body, and soul. Physical healing, which refers to the body, is defined as the process by which the cells in the body regenerate or repair themselves. During the repair or regeneration stage, the damage or burden area is reduced.

Spiritual healing is a set of beliefs that involves faith bringing about healing through prayers or rituals that evoke the presence of divine healing. Christians, of course, believe in spiritual healing. In prayer, God's authority is proclaimed and demonstrated through the freedom from bondage or infirmity.

The spirit part of man can also be afflicted or vexed, requiring divine intervention. Spiritual healing is required for deliverance as well as self-improvement during the process of self-actualization. Spiritual healing actually treats the whole person—soul, spirit, and body.

Modern science categorizes spiritual healing as a form of alternative medicine. Modern science has defined spiritual healing as a means of treating disease through the process of an individual seeking enlightenment or meaning in life. The basis of this way of thinking is a belief that one has an experience with a divine power and/or belief that the ailment was assigned to him or her for a greater purpose.

Let's look at what scripture says about healing. "Beloved, I wish above all things that thou mayest prosper and be in health, even as thy soul prospereth" (3 John 1:2). Health is a mirror of our soul. The soul is made up of the will, mind, and emotions. How we see, feel about, and think about life is how we view health. Positive thoughts, positive views on life, and positive views on one's self reflect the health of one's soul.

> And when Joseph came home, they brought him the present which was in their hand into the house, and bowed themselves to the earth. And he asked them of their welfare, and said, Is your father well, the old man of whom ye spake? Is he yet alive? And they answered, Thy servant our father is in good health, he is yet alive. And they bowed down their heads, and made obeisance. (Genesis 43:26–28)

As we see, the boy's father was in good health. If we study the chapter, the setting occurred during a severe famine in Egypt (Genesis 43:1). Yet he was in good health because he is alive and without sickness.

Let's take another look at scripture and how our souls reflect our health. "A sound heart is the life of the flesh: but envy the rottenness of the bones" (Proverbs 14:30). We begin to see the doorway to diseases and condition of the body. A sound heart—a heart of peace, understanding, and contentment—reflects on our bodies as the "life of the flesh." One's body will reflect the condition of the heart or emotional part of man.

Let's take a brief look at emotional eaters. A heavy heart—or a heart full of despair, sadness, and hopelessness—often produces a heavy body. A heavy body or an obese state reflects excess baggage or excess weight that is not only carried in the body as fat but in the soul as weight, pressure, or loss of control.

What Is Healing?

Healing is not a group of words that we profess with our mouths and do not believe in our hearts. Some people say, "I believe God will heal me one day."

We should never put off for tomorrow what we can do today. Healing is God's specialty. He can heal any type of disease. Some people say, "It is God's will for me to be sick." It is not God's will for any of us to be sick or lost. Review the following examples from the Bible:

> "Therefore I say unto you, Take no thought for your life, what ye shall eat, or what ye shall drink; nor yet for your body, what ye shall put on. Is not the life more than meat, and the body than raiment? Therefore take no thought, saying, What shall we eat? or, What shall we drink? or, Wherewithal shall we be clothed? (For after all these things do the Gentiles seek:) for your heavenly Father knoweth that ye have need of all these things. But seek ye first the kingdom of God, and his righteousness; and all these things shall be added unto you" (Matthew 6:25, 6:31–33).

> "Be careful for nothing; but in every thing by prayer and supplication with thanksgiving let your requests be made known unto God. And the peace of God, which passeth all understanding, shall keep your hearts and minds through Christ Jesus" (Philippians 4:6–7).

> "The soul of the sluggard desireth, and hath nothing: but the soul of the diligent shall be made fat" (Proverbs 13:4).

> "For I will restore health unto thee, and I will heal thee of thy wounds, saith the Lord" (Jeremiah 30:17).

> "Many are the afflictions of the righteous: but the Lord delivereth him out of them all" (Psalm 34:19).

How Does Healing Come?

True healing occurs gradually. It involves a process. Complete healing of a man involves healing in the spirit, soul, and body. Can we receive a partial healing? To have a partial healing is like saying God is not capable of completion. Many people mistake being free of symptoms for being completely healed. Being free of symptoms is a blessing, but being truly healed involves closing the door that allowed the disease to come in. Remember that God is a god of order and completion.

A person who is depressed, sad, lethargic, or negative can receive a blessing and be set free from the symptoms of depression. He or she will feel good, have a positive outlook, and be more energetic. But as soon as a test or trial comes, that feeling is gone—and the depression resurfaces. Is this true healing?

In order for the person to experience true healing and remain free from depression, several things must take place. The first thing is to identify the source of the depression. The source of all mental illness originates in the soul. Second, we must understand what the soul consists of and find possible causes for the mental illness. When operating in the gift of healing, God reveals the demons that cause the depression, and he reveals the source of how the demons gained access to infect that part of your soul:

> "The spirit of a man will sustain his infirmity; but a wounded spirit who can bear?" (Proverbs 18:14).

> "He (God) helps the brokenhearted and binds their wounds" (Psalm 147:3).

The spirit is the source of the sickness and is sustained or maintained based on the condition of the spirit. If God does not dwell in your spirit and your internal state is negative, your external state will mirror the image the spirit is projecting.

In Psalm 147:3, God says he will help or heal the brokenhearted and bind their wounds. God deals with the source, the heart (the "soulish" part of man), and then binds up the wounds that are a result of the broken heart (sickness, disease, etc.).

In order to bring about true healing, he first heals the source. It is through the source that the door is opened to spirits that traffic in us, bind us, and set up kingdoms. The evil spirit will speak to the mind, causing the person to see what is spoken to him or her. The evil spirit's voice becomes louder than God's voice. This causes the individual to begin to speak things that may not actually be. This may cause symptoms of what was spoken in the mind by the evil spirit.

The physical realm is a mirror of the spiritual realm. If you have chaotic thoughts, negative feelings, and constant internal battles, the world around you will shape and conform to the world that is inside you. Why? When we are overwhelmed by negative emotions or feelings that are secondary to any disappointment or grief we may be experiencing, the heart begins to speak from this negative place. Speaking negative thoughts brings negative results. We should speak what we want to see. We should not speak what is shown to us or told to us if it is contrary to God's word.

> "Many are the afflictions of the righteous: but the Lord delivereth him out of them all" (Psalm 34:19).

There will always be periods of ups and downs, negatives and positives, good and evil, pain and joy. There will always be God. There will always be good. As long as we are awaiting the return of Christ, there will always be evil because there is still Satan.

Definition of a Miracle

According to *Wikipedia*, a miracle is an unexpected event attributed to a divine agent. I love this concept of something unexpected that manifests immediately.

This is like a fig tree dying overnight, water turning to wine, or feeding five thousand people with two fishes and five loaves of bread. A miracle happens instantly while healing comes gradually. A person on his or her deathbed, with pain raging as daggers are thrown from miles away into a bull's-eye, suddenly and instantly can be free of all pain after a prayer. A person whose heart stopped suddenly awakens with a stronger heartbeat and can speak after a prayer. These are miracles of healing. What if you are alone and a dog with rabies is charging after you, ready to strike like lightning? Imagine saying "Leave here now!" The dog will stop dead in its tracks, whimper, and run away. Having the power to command a raging dog could be considered a miracle. These are miracles that have occurred immediately following words of scriptures. To perform miracles, one must have obtained the gift of miracles! Such phenomena cannot occur without the gift. This gift only comes through fasting and praying.

Fasting brings down strongholds. Strongholds are belief systems that have formed walls around a learned or ingrained belief that is contrary to God's word. These strongholds are the roots of our subconscious. A stronghold that is formed will govern physical behavior and is capable of producing results that this negative belief system is formulated in. They are the unknowns that the Bible tells us to "cast down" or throw away. They are capable of producing results in the physical realm.

Strongholds are actual doorways into our spirits. They are spirits on the battleground during the war between good and evil. The subconscious is the doorway when our souls become full of certain beliefs. The belief spills over into the subconscious where the pressure forces the door to open, and it flows into our spirits. When the door is shut, our conscious mind is no longer aware of the stronghold's origin and results in our actions contradicting God's word.

Generational curses are strongholds. A disease, such as breast cancer, can live in a woman's subconscious mind, causing her to fear the disease. From a spiritual view, we see it embedded in the subconscious mind before the disease develops. Breast cancer affects mostly women. The goal of breast cancer is to eradicate the population. Breasts are like jewels to men and are satisfying, according to the Book of Solomon. They produce milk to feed our offspring. Milk is food for newborn babies, but the devil will interrupt our life cycles in any way he can.

Chapter 3

Man

According to the Bible, man is made in the image of God:

"And God said, Let us make man in our image, after our likeness: and let them have dominion over the fish of the sea, and over the fowl of the air, and over the cattle, and over all the earth, and over every creeping thing that creepeth upon the earth" (Genesis 1:26).

The first part of this passage says, "Let us." God is complete. The scripture states that God is the Alpha and the Omega, the beginning and the end. "And he said unto me, It is done. I am Alpha and Omega, the beginning and the end" (Revelation 21:6).

God is spirit (the beginning), thus the first part of man is spirit. We were in God and in the mind of God before we were formed (Genesis 1:27).

God created man in his own image. The word "create" can be defined as bringing something into existence. Thus, we were first created or brought into existence in the image of God or as a spirit! The first recipe of man is the substance of creativity. Our will, mind, and emotions were birthed from the mind, will, and emotions of God. Our souls were created first. The soul has the power to create, dominate, and rule. Our souls were formed in God's authority and his ability to create. The second part of man is the body or our flesh.

"And the Lord God formed man of the dust of the ground, and breathed into his nostrils the breath of life; and man became a living soul" (Genesis 2:7).

Our bodies were formed from the dust of the ground. We were first created, and then we were formed. The word "formed" can be defined as "to shape or give structure." Our flesh or bodies were formed from the dust. This doesn't mean we are created from the dirt we walk on every day. The same dust that was used to form the stars is the same dust we were created from. Dust is a single particle; a group of particles of one kind is an object of sorts. Clouds are an example of this.

The third part of man was created when God breathed the breath into man—and man became a living soul. Thus, life, the spirit, was placed in a created soul that was wrapped in flesh formed from dust.

Let's recap the components of man. Man is composed of the body, soul, and spirit. I love the way my pastor calls us a speaking spirit that lives in a body that possesses a soul. Pastor Anthony Q. Knotts of the Embassy Church International reminds us often that we are a speaking spirit.

We can define man as a created being—formed from dust—that possesses the breath of God and was created in his image.

We must journey a little deeper into each component of man before we can discuss the "afflictions" of man. I want to take time to look at each part of man and give biblical scriptures for each part.

Chapter 4
The Body

Our bodies, or our "flesh," as we see them, were formed from dust. Freedictionary.com defines dust as "a fine, dry particle of matter." So we are billions and billions of fine, dry particles of matter originating from the same place.

The body is also composed of 60–70 percent water. Depending on the health of the individual, the percentage can be more. Babies have a greater percentage than adult men do. Adult men have a greater percentage than adult women do, and people with excessive body fat have a lower percentage of water. The lean muscle (a sign of health) is capable of storing a greater amount of water than fat can. Women have more fat tissue than men do. Men tend to have less water in their bodies.

Before God created man, he created the heavens and the earth. Before he planted, God created every plant and herb, and there was no need for rain because there was "no man" created to till the ground.

> And every plant of the field before it was in the earth, and
> every herb of the field before it grew: For the Lord God
> had not caused it to rain upon the earth, and there was
> not a man to till the ground. (Genesis 2:5)

The earth was complete before he dressed it. The rain was not needed because rain falls or descends. "But there went up a mist from the earth, and watered the whole face of the ground" (Genesis 2:6).

Thus, man was complete when he created us because we were created in the image of God. I call it the "completeness" of God. The body, like earth, has water that flows up and out. The Bible calls this "water" a fountain that springs from the belly or the spirit. "He that believeth on me, as the scripture hath said, out of his belly shall flow rivers of living water" (John 7:38).

When Adam and Eve sinned, this "living water" dried up. God also cursed the ground, causing the waters to dry up. By this, Adam shall eat bread by working the ground so hard he shall sweat. "Cursed is the ground for thy sake; in sorrow shalt thou eat of it all the days of thy life" (Genesis 3:17).

"In the sweat of thy face shalt thou eat bread, till thou return unto the ground; for out of it wast thou taken: for dust thou art, and unto dust shalt thou return" (Genesis 3:19). The earth is symbolic of the body. Cursed grounds bring cursed fruits or roots that bear no fruits.

Our bodies and our flesh were sentenced to death when Adam and Eve sinned. Diseases that originate in the body or flesh were rooted or "traded" into us when Adam traded dominion of the earth for wisdom of this world with Satan.

Diseases that originate in the flesh are cursed. We see examples of curses in the body when God cursed Pharaoh and his people with boils (Exodus 9:9), leprosy (Numbers 12:10), and hemorrhoids (Deuteronomy 28:27). Some examples of modern-day curses of the flesh are AIDS, leprosy, hemorrhoids, and autoimmune diseases such as rheumatoid arthritis and lupus. The curse is designed to "return" the body back to the ground.

Autoimmune diseases are caused when the body's immune system attacks the body. These are generational curses that have no natural cures. A great example is rheumatoid arthritis. This is a disease of the joints. The body's immune system begins to break down the cartilage and joints of the body. Common places are the hands and knees. "The Lord shall smite thee in the knees, and in the legs, with a sore botch that cannot be healed" (Deuteronomy 28:35).

Another autoimmune disease is lupus. This is a collection of diseases with similar underlying problems. A symptom of lupus is cutaneous lupus erythematosus, which is characterized by lesions on the skin that tend to follow sun exposure. The body's immune system attacks the skin with lupus; the body will attack organs, skin, and joints of the body. The most common symptoms are joint pain, skin rash, and fever.

Autoimmune diseases are hereditary. Any hereditary disease is a generational curse passed from parent to child. The child will either develop the curse or pass it to his or her offspring where it will be carried or manifested. Another example of a curse whose origin is in the body is sickle-cell anemia. Sickle-cell anemia is a hereditary blood disease where the body makes crescent-shaped red blood cells. Normal red blood cells are disc-shaped. Picture a doughnut without a hole in the center. These normal red blood cells move through our blood vessels without difficulty. Sickle cells are sticky and tend to block blood flow. The blocked blood flow can cause serious infection, organ damage, and pain.

Blood is symbolic of life. The normal lifespan of a red blood cell is 120 days. Sickle cells only live between ten and twenty days. This causes anemia, a blood condition in which the body has a low number of red blood cells. The bone marrow is unable to produce red blood cells to replace the rapidly dying sickle cells. Sickle-cell anemia is a generational curse with symptoms of pain.

It is safe to say that generational curses of the body have the same symptoms. "The Lord shall smite thee with a consumption, and with a fever, and with an inflammation, and with an extreme burning, and with the sword, and with blasting, and with mildew; and they shall pursue thee until thou perish" (Deuteronomy 28:22).

As we have seen with these examples, some diseases that originate in the body will produce symptoms that cause some type of inflammation or mild fever. Inflammation in the joints or leg can cause a rise in body temperature or fever. "The Lord shall smite thee in the knees, and in the legs" (Deuteronomy 28:35).

13

CHAPTER 5
The Soul

The soul or soulish part of man consists of the will, the mind, and emotions. It is what Satan desires to spoil.

"Behold, all souls are mine; as the soul of the father, so also the soul of the son is mine: the soul that sinneth, it shall die" (Ezekiel 18:4).

The Will

The first part of man's soul I would like to discuss is man's will. Every person has a free will. We have the ability to make decisions and choices based on our ability to reason and judge. This innate ability is the gift of God. It is one of the many characteristics of God. God is such a gentleman that he never goes against man's will or his choices.

Man was designed to love, worship, and cocreate, according to the purpose that was placed within us by God. By definition, a man's will is the apparent ability to make choices "free" from certain kinds of constraints. In other words, man is able to make choices without the influences of external or internal constraints—rather than based on one's own perception of what is and what isn't.

> "I call heaven and earth to record this day against you, that
> I have set before you life and death, blessing and cursing:
> therefore choose life, that both thou and thy seed may
> live" (Deuteronomy 30:19).

"And if it seem evil unto you to serve the Lord, choose
you this day whom ye will serve; whether the gods which
your fathers served that were on the other side of the
flood, or the gods of the Amorites, in whose land ye dwell:
but as for me and my house, we will serve the Lord."
(Joshua 24:15).

"That if thou shalt confess with thy mouth the Lord Jesus,
and shalt believe in thine heart that God hath raised him
from the dead, thou shalt be saved." (Romans 10:9).

The will of man is what I like to say is the beauty of us. Humans
have the right to choose life or death, good or evil, and freedom or
bondage.

God lays before man the choice to serve him or Satan. He
paints the picture of the consequences of both, as we saw in
Deuteronomy 30:19.

The Mind

The mind of man is complex. Oceans of words flow together and
interpret the pictures and reflections of life. The mind contains
the doors between the dimensions of man, the doors between the
conscious and the subconscious, and the doors between the body and
soul and soul and spirit.

The purpose of man's mind is to store information and facts. It
is constantly recording our experiences. When external experiences
flood our minds, our minds process and reprocess them until they
are pushed further into our subconscious by new experiences. In the
beginning—before we were created—we were in the mind of God.
This approach was the original pattern of man's mind before the fall
of Adam.

God is a spirit first. He became the Word, and then he became
flesh. Likewise, we were spirit (because we were in God) before we
became a product of God's words. "God said, Let us make man"

(Genesis 1:26). We came into existence because God did not just speak the word—he created it as well. We were designed to think and process information originally from the inward parts of man.

Adam's fall in the Garden of Eden—his spiritual death—resulted in man's mind becoming "carnal" or deriving and storing information based on experiences of external environments and our flesh. This "carnal" mind forces thinking to become processed from an outside approach instead of God's original mind of an "inside" approach. In other words, things that bring the spirit death (inside) are not felt in our spirit until the experience has consumed our bodies, our soul, and our spirit. This outside approach brings disease and sickness after we define and deal with our emotions.

Worldly Mind

There are two types of minds: the worldly mind and the godly mind. The worldly mind or the "carnal" mind is the mind of the flesh. "For they that are after the flesh do mind the things of the flesh; but they that are after the Spirit the things of the Spirit. For to be carnally minded is death; but to be spiritually minded is life and peace" (Romans 8:5-6).

When we look at the word *mind* in verses 5 and 6, it is "phroneo." According to *Strong's Concordance*, it means "intensively to interest one's self in (with concern or obedience set the affection on)." The word *mind* in verse 7 is "phronema," which means to purpose. To be carnally minded is to choose to intensively put one's interest in self or purposely use affection for serving the flesh. Sinners choose to serve themselves and things of pleasure pertaining to themselves rather than serving God. Another way to look at this is as a selfish mind-set.

"They that are after the Spirit, the things of the Spirit" purposely serve the things of the spirit or things of God. To be spiritually minded is not a selfish state and denies one's self to follow after the things of God.

"Set your affection on things above, not on things on the earth" (Colossians 3:2).

"That ye put off concerning the former conversation the old man, which is corrupt according to the deceitful lusts; And be renewed in the spirit of your mind" (Ephesians 4:22–23).

"This I say then, Walk in the Spirit, and ye shall not fulfil the lust of the flesh" (Galatians 5:16).

The Emotions

The emotional part of the soul is the part that involves feelings. Our emotions allow us to feel love, hate, joy, sadness, peace, and anger. Emotions are necessary because they allow us to interact with each other as humans. God is a God of relationship. Our emotions allow us to be connected to one another as a whole.

Emotions have purpose in the walk with God—if our emotions are rooted and grounded in his word. In other words, our emotions should allow us to produce the fruit of the spirit, based on our ability to produce the two primary basic emotions: love and hate. Without emotions, there cannot be soil for the fruits of the spirit. In order to bear the fruits of the spirit, we must have the ability to produce emotion. A sick soul or a dead soul loses the ability to feel love. The soul without love has a stony or cold heart. The soul is emotionless.

> "But the fruit of the Spirit is love, joy, peace, longsuffering, gentleness, goodness, faith" (Galatians 5:22).
>
> "And above all things have fervent charity among yourselves: for charity shall cover the multitude of sins" (1 Peter 4:8).
>
> "If any man love not the Lord Jesus Christ, let him be Anathema Maranatha" (1 Corinthians 16:22).
>
> "I beseech Euodias, and beseech Syntyche, that they be of the same mind in the Lord" (Philippians 4:2).

A spiritual mind allows love to birth the fruits of the spirit. Carnal mind is self-pleasure. It can only produce hate, envy, jealousy, strife, bitterness, and sadness.

"For ye are yet carnal: for whereas there is among you envying, and strife, and divisions, are ye not carnal, and walk as men?" (1 Corinthians 3:3).

"Now the works of the flesh are manifest, which are these; Adultery, fornication, uncleanness, lasciviousness, Idolatry, witchcraft, hatred, variance, emulations, wrath, strife, seditions, heresies, Envyings, murders, drunkenness, revellings, and such like" (Galatians 5:19–21).

"And fear not them which kill the body, but are not able to kill the soul: but rather fear him which is able to destroy both soul and body in hell" (Matthew 10:28).

We have to understand the soul. The world's system understands that, in order to get to a person's mind, you have to get to him or her through his or her emotions. We experience pain or pleasure when we engage in certain behaviors. If the stimulation is pain, it is natural for us to seek a substitute for the pain. Something that causes pleasure often replaces the pain. For example, if someone is an addict or engages in addictive behavior, it is because the addictive behavior causes short-term pleasure. The pleasure at that moment causes the addict to forget the pain, and he or she continues the behavior. Addiction is a symptom of a bigger problem. We must change the way we view the addiction in order to overcome the addiction. We must see that long-term pain is not worth short-term pleasure.

If someone you love is suffering from an addiction, you must understand that some type of internal pain drove him or her to replace the pain with whatever he or she is addicted to. The internal pain must be dealt with, acknowledged, accepted, and healed through God's words in prayer. God's words and promises in his scriptures must be used to fill the void he or she is desperately trying to fill with the addiction.

Chapter 6
The Spirit

When looking into the spirit of man, we must first try to define the spirit. The spirit is the breath of God. Every living soul has a spirit that originates from God.

When God breathed into Adam, he gave Adam the breath of life (Genesis 2:7). This breath of life is the spirit part of man. The spirit part of man died in the Garden of Eden. When the spirit of Adam and Eve died, it no longer qualified them to remain in the Garden of Eden (Genesis 3:23–24). This spiritual death closed the door between man and God and opened the door to spiritual death. Anything dead births disease, sickness, and decay.

"And the Lord God formed man of the dust of the ground, and breathed into his nostrils the breath of life; and man became a living soul" (Genesis 2:7).

"Therefore the Lord God sent him forth from the garden of Eden, to till the ground from whence he was taken. So he drove out the man; and he placed at the east of the garden of Eden Cherubims, and a flaming sword which turned every way, to keep the way of the tree of life" (Genesis 3:23–24).

The Dwellings of Man

When God created man, he placed man in the Garden of Eden (Genesis 2:15). The Garden of Eden was earth when it was created.

It was the first dwelling place for man to commune with God (Genesis 2:16).

Man was created in the image of God. Man was a speaking spirit. God gave Adam the commandment to name every beast and tree and to eat freely. But of the tree of knowledge of good and evil man should not eat (Genesis 2:16–17). The purpose of the Garden of Eden was to produce man since he was created from its dust (Genesis 2:7) to supply food (Genesis 2:9) and to populate the earth (Genesis 1:28). Most importantly, the Garden of Eden was a place where God and man could fellowship.

> "And the Lord God commanded the man, saying, Of every tree of the garden thou mayest freely eat" (Genesis 2:16).

> "But of the tree of the knowledge of good and evil, thou shalt not eat" (Genesis 2:17).

> "And out of the ground made the Lord God to grow every tree that is pleasant to the sight, and good for food" (Genesis 2:9).

In Genesis 2:21–22, the Lord God caused a deep sleep to fall upon Adam. While he slept, God took one of his ribs and closed up the flesh. The Lord God took the rib from Adam and made a woman.

Satan was in the garden with man. He removed man from the garden to take his authority as cocreator, to take our dominion, and to hurt God. The Garden of Eden represents safety. This was a place for our hedge of protection. It was a place where man and God had an indirect relationship with each other.

Satan wanted to have advantage over us (2 Corinthians 2:11). He was the son of the morning light (Isaiah 14:12). He was God's worshipping angel. His fall was the reason we were created—to take his place as God's worshipper!

We must understand our purpose as God's dwelling place! He desires to dwell among his people and in his servants. How can he comfort us if we do not allow his spirit to dwell and reside within us? Do we even know who we are? I want you to ask yourself three questions:

1. What was I created for?
2. Who controls me and my surroundings?
3. What is it that dwells in me?

> "Lest Satan should get an advantage of us: for we are not ignorant of his devices" (2 Corinthians 2:11).

> "How art thou fallen from heaven, O Lucifer, son of the morning!" (Isaiah 14:12).

When we are in direct relationship with God, we are healthy in our spirit, body, and soul. The scripture does not speak of disease, curses, or sickness until Adam was commanded to leave the garden.

The Garden of Eden is symbolic of the perfect will of God. The Garden of Eden is the hedge of protection that God placed around man to keep him safe. In the Book of Job, Satan asked permission to touch Job. He stated that Job was protected from Satan's army only because of the hedge of protection that was around Job and his family (Job 1:10).

"Hast not thou made an hedge about him, and about his house, and about all that he hath on every side? thou hast blessed the work of his hands, and his substance is increased in the land" (Job 1:10).

The Tabernacle

After the fall of man, God wanted to dwell with his people. He still wanted that close fellowship with his children.

God needed a dwelling place consecrated from his spirit. God gave the pattern and instruction for the tabernacle. "And let them make me a sanctuary; that I may dwell among them. According to all that I shew thee, after the pattern of the tabernacle, and the pattern of all the instruments thereof, even so shall ye make it" (Exodus 25:8–9).

The original tabernacle was built by people, according to God's instruction. In this tabernacle, there were the outer courts, inner courts, and holy of holies. Again, we find no sickness, diseases, or curses in the tabernacle. One place was the holy of holies.

God's spirit dwelt in the holy of holies. Apply this to our bodies. The holies of holies are our spirits. Since Jesus came and made salvation available to mankind, we are at liberty to dwell in the same place as God. This is why the tabernacle is our bodies (2 Corinthians 6:16).

The purpose of God making us his new tabernacle or "temple" is to dwell within us, walk in us, and be our God. Our living temple is to house the spirit of God, protect our destiny, and to provide comfort as God did for Adam before he placed enmity between man and woman. This enmity is the door in the soul where loneliness causes room for the root of jealousy and the fruits of bitterness and envy!

"To the one we are the savour of death unto death; and to the other the savour of life unto life. And who is sufficient for these things?" (2 Corinthians 2:16).

"And I will put enmity between thee and the woman, and between thy seed and her seed; it shall bruise thy head, and thou shalt bruise his heel" (Genesis 3:15).

"Blessed are they that mourn: for they shall be comforted" (Matthew 5:4).

"But when the Comforter is come, whom I will send unto you from the Father, even the Spirit of truth, which proceedeth from the Father, he shall testify of me" (John 15:26).

"Who comforteth us in all our tribulation, that we may be able to comfort them which are in any trouble, by the comfort wherewith we ourselves are comforted of God" (2 Corinthians 1:4).

The place of worship we call "church" is a place where the believer can come and receive faith. Our walk with God and our salvation is by faith not by sight (2 Corinthians 5:7).

We must not forsake the assembly or coming together of the saints. Where there is unity, there is strength. The scriptures are loaded with reasons why we should fellowship with one another. God promises us that where there are two or three gathered in his name, he will be in the midst. God is where his anointing is.

Can you find anywhere in scripture where someone was healed outside the presence of God? There must be a move on our behalf into the presence of God before true healing can be received. The church (another dwelling of God) is a place where God can dwell with his people as a group.

"For we walk by faith, not by sight" (2 Corinthians 5:7).

"Not forsaking the assembling of ourselves together, as the manner of some is" (Hebrews 10:25).

"Behold, how good and how pleasant it is for brethren to dwell together in unity! It is like the precious ointment upon the head, that ran down upon the beard, even Aaron's beard: that went down to the skirts of his garments" (Psalm 133:1–2).

We must not isolate ourselves when we are in need of healing. The devil doesn't want us to become delivered. When we are faced with sickness, why do we withhold the information from our loved ones and friends? In doing so, the sickness grows until we cannot contain it. That is when we begin to speak about what is growing in us!

CHAPTER 7
Disease of the Soul

Now that we have a foundation of what man is and what healing is, let's put it all together. I want to take the time to discuss the disease or sickness of the soul, the cure, and the scriptures.

The soul is devised of the will, mind, and emotions. The disease or sickness of the soul is rooted in strong negative emotions of bitterness, envy, strife, and anger. The ruling spirit is the spirit of fear and the spirit of pride. All mental illnesses are rooted in the spirit of fear.

Healing of the soul consists of bringing one's will, mind, and emotions to an agreement. A person can spend lots of money on clothes, food, and entertainment—and still be severely depressed. Another person can laugh at inappropriate things and still weep.

It takes a mind to serve God. Paul says, "Let this mind be in you, which was also in Christ Jesus" (Philippians 2:5). A damaged soul leads to double-mindedness. Double-minded individuals are divided within themselves and are unstable in all their ways (James 1:8).

Sins that bring damage to the soul are sexual immorality, rejection, jealousy, and anger within one's self. The soul can be healed through fasting and prayer accompanied by meditation on the Bible.

Meditation on God's word is a requirement for maintaining complete healing and deliverance. The spirit is infinite. How else can one's spirit house ten thousand demons? We must receive wise counsel through his word in order to have instructions for our life.

Affliction means something that causes great suffering. Mental illness can have diverse effects for the afflicted and the person's family. When we look deeper into mental illness, one would think that it originates in the soulish realm. This may not always be the case. One could develop depression from head trauma, but the manifestation will still be seen in the person's emotions.

The scriptures are filled with defenses and spiritual warfare against mental illness. The devil's desire is to turn us away from God. Man was designed to be in a relationship with God. When man has no relationship with God, there is a void. People try to fill this void on a conscious level and on a subconscious level. The need to be loved and give love is part of man's makeup. We were designed to receive love and to give love to God. Without God's love in us, it is almost impossible to withstand the stresses of everyday living. Some may go through life with more highs than lows, but most people have ways of coping with anger, disappointment, or sadness.

To get to the heart of mental illness, we must look at the ruling spirits: the spirit of fear, the spirit of pride, the spirit of deafness and dumbness, and the spirit of whoredom. Each spirit attacks our soulish realm. The manifestation or the "fruit" may be different, but they all produce the same results. The result is death of the soul. Without a soul—or the mind, will, and emotions—man becomes useless to himself, others, and God. A dead soul cannot give God glory or worship him.

The spirit of fear causes us to doubt, hate, kill, steal, destroy, and become lacking. When fear attacks our minds, it causes us to feel inadequate, incomplete, and paranoid. The ruling spirit of all compulsive disorders is fear.

Compulsive disorders become compulsive because of the need to control a perceived expected outcome. Compulsive liars lie because they are afraid of others finding out how they really feel about themselves. Regardless of what the lie is, the root is fear.

Compulsive hand-washers are afraid that they will "remain dirty." This drives them to continue the compulsive activity. The root is fear. Fear can creep in from childhood as learned behavior or as generational curses.

The spirit of pride produces rebellion, bitterness, envy, and strife. Some anxiety disorders and certain forms of cancer are ruled by the spirit of pride. People whose motivations are rooted or governed by the spirit of pride have issues with bonding and selfishness. Their discussions are often based on one's perception of self and are not a team effort.

People with pure motives can err by this spirit: A husband loses his job, but he doesn't allow his family to seek assistance. When the family does, he withdraws and becomes intimidated. His feelings are kept inside, which eventually leads to the behaviors such as excessive drinking, smoking, or isolation from the wife and children. Does this sound familiar?

The spirit of whoredom rules all sexual immoralities. This spirit also may manifest as greed, gluttony, addiction, or an obsession with vanity. This ruling spirit's goal is to destroy the soul—and destroy it quickly!

The ruling spirit of deafness and dumbness is a strong man who is defeated only through much fasting and prayer. This fruit of the spirit affects the person's behavior. Medical disorders such as epilepsy and inner ear disorders are governed by this spirit. Suicide, borderline personality disorder, schizophrenia, blindness, and narcolepsy are fruits of this spirit.

The soul's enemy is our own consciousness, including negative thoughts about the self. The soul consists of the will, the mind, and emotions. How often do we find ourselves engaging in self-destructive behaviors, such as overeating, drug use, or multiple sex partners? We justify these behaviors by claiming that we are just having fun, but these are emotion-driven behaviors.

Healing the Soul

When ministering to a soulish disease, one must understand the composition of the soul, the purpose of the soul, and the value of the soul as it pertains to God. The root of the ruling spirit must be cast out. Attacking the fruit does not destroy the spirit. The ruling spirit root must be exposed—and then cast out by purification of his word.

The principles of replacement are important in spiritual warfare. The gift of casting out demons must be in operating as well as the gift of healings. I have composed a list of mental disorders, their ruling spirits and fruits, and how to be delivered from these ailments.

Bipolar Disorder

Spiritually, the ruling spirit behind bipolar disorder is the "deaf and dumb" spirit. The fruit or symptom produced by this disorder is severe mood disturbances that interfere with life, including severe depression or extreme excitement. Deliverance can occur when one is set free from this evil spirit. Cast out the deaf and dumb spirit as Jesus did in Mark 5:1–20. Replace this spirit with the spirit "of power, and of love, and of a sound mind" (2 Timothy 1:7).

Bipolar disorder is a generational curse. To stop this illness from affecting the individual's future generations, a forty-day fast should be accompanied by deliverance. Jesus fasted for forty days before he went to the cross because every curse and stronghold for those after him was broken. Jesus came that we might have life and have life more abundantly (John 10:10).

Schizophrenia

- A mental disorder characterized by loss of contact with reality, symptoms of delusions, incoherence, hallucinations, and breaks in thought processes.
- Primary origin is the soulish realm.
- Fruits are manifested in the mind of the individual as delusions, breaks in thought processes, paranoia, etc.
- Ruling spirit is the deaf and dumb spirit.
- To be delivered, cast out the ruling spirit (deaf and dumb) through binding and loose the spirit of power, love, and sound mind (2 Timothy 1:7).
- This generational curse can be broken with a forty-day fast. Meditate on scriptures that reference the mind day and night.
- "Thou wilt keep him in perfect peace, whose mind is stayed on thee: because he trusteth in thee" (Isaiah 26:3).
- "Let this mind be in you, which was also in Christ Jesus" (Philippians 2:5).

- "And the peace of God, which passeth all understanding, shall keep your hearts and minds through Christ Jesus. Finally, brethren, whatsoever things are true, whatsoever things are honest, whatsoever things are just, whatsoever things are pure, whatsoever things are lovely, whatsoever things are of good report; if there be any virtue, and if there be any praise, think (meditate) on these things" (Philippians 4:7–8).

Seizures

- A sudden episode of transit neurologic symptoms, such as involuntary muscle movements, sensory disturbances, and altered consciousness.
- Origin is of the body or soul (the mind or brain).
- Ruling spirit is deaf and dumb.
- Fruits manifested in the body.
- Deliverance—cast out deaf and dumb spirit through binding; loose the spirit of power, love, and sound mind; and meditate on all scriptures of the mind as above and on healing.
- "Bless the Lord, O my soul and forget not his benefits: Who forgiveth all thine iniquities; who healeth all thy diseases" (Psalm 103:2–3).
- "But he was wounded for our transgressions, he was bruised for our iniquities: the chastisement of our peace was upon him; and with his stripes we are healed" (Isaiah 53:5).
- "Who his own self bare our sins in his own body on the tree, that we, being dead to sins, should live unto righteousness; by whose stripes ye were healed" (1 Peter 2:24).

Depression

- May be described as sadness or feeling "blue." It is a sense of hopelessness.
- Origin is of the soul.

- Fruits manifested first in the mind and then the body as tiredness, a decrease or increase in appetite, and an inability to concentrate.
- Ruling spirit is fear. "Men's hearts failing them for fear" (Luke 21:26).
- Deliverance—cast out the spirit of fear through binding and meditate on scriptures that reference hope and deliverance.
- "And now, Lord, what wait I for? my hope is in thee" (Psalm 39:7).
- "And be not conformed to this world: but be ye transformed by the renewing of your mind, that ye may prove what is that good, and acceptable, and perfect, will of God" (Romans 12:2).
- "Wherefore gird up the loins of your mind, be sober, and hope to the end for the grace that is to be brought unto you at the revelation of Jesus Christ" (1 Peter 1:13).
- "Be of good courage, and he shall strengthen your heart, all ye that hope in the Lord" (Psalm 31:24).
- "Wait on the Lord: be of good courage, and he shall strengthen thine heart: wait, I say, on the Lord" (Psalm 27:14).

All mental illnesses, including sexual immortality, originate in the soul. These illnesses are ruled by pride and self-destruction.

Here is an example of a general prayer you can use when delivering the soul. The parentheses give instruction and rationale for what you are praying about. You may allow God to lead you, and he may give you your own prayer. This general prayer is based upon Holy Scripture:

> Father, in the name of Jesus, I bind the spirit of (name of spirit, Matthew 16:19) and loose it (must send the spirit back to whence it came from, Luke 11:24) back to dry places seeking rest and finding none. I release the spirit of power, love, and sound mind. I cast out all unclean, wicked, and evil spirits and command them to come out in Jesus's name (John 14:13). "I am come that they might

> have life, and that they might have it more abundantly"
> (John 10:10). According to Psalm 44:4, I command
> deliverance for (your/their) life. I thank you, God, for
> complete healing and deliverance according to your word
> (Isaiah 53:5). In Jesus' name (John 14:13). Amen.

The soul is precious to God. It is the seat or throne of our hearts. We can only love and do ministry with a complete, healed soul. The only brokenness that the oil of joy flows through is our will!

We can only be whole through knowledge of him. We can only remain whole through a relationship with him. We can only remain full of joy when we are filled with him. Let us not live our lives in defeat.

The savior was slain so that we could have life and live more abundantly.

CHAPTER 8
Diseases of the Spirit

The spirit of man contains the spirit of God. Our spirit was breathed into us the moment God breathed into Adam's nostrils. The Hebrew word *neshamah* is translated as "breath" in Genesis 2:7. It is translated as "spirit" in Proverbs 20:27. This word speaks of the spirit of man. To sum it all up, the breath of God in man is the spirit.

In my research, I found that the spirit can also be composed of three parts: the conscience, the fellowship, and the intuition. The conscience determines right or wrong.

God relates to us through our fellowship with him. We know what is of God because of our intuition.

"I lie not, my conscience also bearing me witness in the Holy Ghost" (Romans 9:1). Our conscience bears witness of God's spirit; according to Romans 8:16, "the Spirit" must witness with our spirit.

John 4:24 tells us that because God is spirit, we must worship him in spirit. Our spirit is where God fellowships or relates with us. Thus, we must know who and what we are fellowshipping with. "For what man knoweth the things of a man, save the spirit of man which is in him?" (1 Corinthians 2:11). It is through intuition in our spirits that we know God.

To bring forth diseases in the spirit is to bring forth death. Afflictions of our spirits are driven to do three things: steer our conscience from God (1 Timothy 4:2), disconnect our fellowship with God (Isaiah 59:1–2), and bring forth confusion where we no longer recognize God because of a reprobated mind (Romans 1:28).

The word *adokimos* in *Strong's Concordance* is translated as "depraved" in the NIV version of Romans 1:28 and "worthless" in the NASB version of Titus 1:16. NKJV translated *adokimos* as "disapproved" in 2 Timothy 3:38.

Paul calls the people godless and wicked men who suppress the truth by their wickedness (Romans 1:28–31). The definition of a reprobate mind is a mind that has become so ingrained in evil that it is not able to stop even in its own best interest (www. modernchristianissues.org). Only God can cure or save one of a "contrite spirit." Man's sin can become so evil that it can cause death of the soul, the spirit, and the body. "The soul that sinneth, it shall die" (Ezekiel 18:4). "For the wages of sin is death" (Romans 6:23).

One can also develop "thorns." I believe these thorns develop in our spirits. They force us to choose between life and death. When the people's burdens entered too close to Moses's heart, he became angry. This thorn caused him to become disobedient. Paul persecuted the church, but as with Moses, God's grace is sufficient. His penalty was only death of his old ways, but had he not chosen life, he would surely have died. His old ways and people became a constant reminder of who he was. He asked God to remove the "thorn" or burden three times (2 Corinthians 12:7–8). Many people argue about what Paul's thorn was; however, when a person is "sick" with sin, God judges.

For deliverance of spiritual sickness, you must confess that you are sinning. You must confess that Jesus is Lord, and you must be willing to cease wicked behaviors. Only God can bring a person to "themselves." One has to spend time talking to God about the "spiritually sick" person instead of spending a lot of time talking to the person. They must confess their sins, repent of their sins, and become reconnected to God. "That if thou shalt confess with thy mouth the Lord Jesus, and shalt believe in thine heart that God hath raised him from the dead, thou shalt be saved" (Romans 10:9).

"And that every tongue should confess that Jesus Christ is Lord, to the glory of God the Father" (Philippians 2:11). To deliver a "sick spirit," you must understand the skill and art of spiritual warfare. The person must be cut off from that which feeds the negative behavior. If the person is suffering from an unhealthy relationship, tell God to "close the door" between them. Then bind the spirit that "drives" them to that behavior. Ask God to open the doors of communication between you and the loved one so that true healing can take place.

Here is a prayer I have used, and I've seen many delivered. The key is to use God's words to fight, and you must put God in remembrance of his word:

> Father, in the name of Jesus, I ask that you close all doors between (name of person) and (unhealthy relationship/ sin) and open all doors of communication between (me) and (them) according to Revelation 3:7–8. Deliver (name) according to Psalm 119:134, and surround (name) with songs of deliverance (Psalm 32:7). I praise you have delivered (name) soul from death and eyes from tears according to Psalm 116:8. I receive miracles of deliverance for (name) life in Jesus's name. Amen.

CHAPTER 9
Fasting

In this chapter, I briefly cover fasting because many books have been written about fasting. Please note that you will need to talk with a physician before you start any fast.

First of all, what exactly is fasting? Merriam-Webster's Online Dictionary describes fasting as "to eat sparingly or to abstain from some foods." Isaiah describes an acceptable fast as to "loose the bands of wickedness, to undo the heavy burdens, and to let the oppressed go free, and that ye break every yoke?" (Isaiah 58:6) "Is it not to deal thy bread to the hungry, and that thou bring the poor that are cast out to thy house? when thou seest the naked, that thou cover him; and that thou hide not thyself from thine own flesh?" (Isaiah 58:7).

"Then shall thy light break forth as the morning, and thine health shall spring forth speedily: and thy righteousness shall go before thee; the glory of the Lord shall be thy reward" (Isaiah 58:8). As we see, there are benefits to fasting.

"Then shalt thou call, and the Lord shall answer; thou shalt cry, and he shall say, Here I am. If thou take away from the midst of thee the yoke, the putting forth of the finger, and speaking vanity" (Isaiah 58:9). These verses cover the spiritual benefits and the health benefits of fasting. Yokes are destroyed, the glory of the Lord is your reward, and prayers are answered speedily. We will always get the answer that we want because he knows what is best for us. "And we know that all things work together for good to them that love God, to them who are the called according to his purpose" (Romans 8:28).

The fourth chapter of the Book of Matthew speaks of Jesus fasting. Jesus fasted for forty days and forty nights. After his fast, he was able to endure the temptations of the tempter. In the wilderness, Jesus did an absolute fast. The scriptures state that when Jesus came down from his fast, he hungered. He went on to do healing in ministry and cast out devils. Jesus also told his disciples that certain things came by fasting and prayer after they asked him why they were not able to perform a certain miracle.

I have done an absolute fast, and I was able to see financial and spiritual miracles. I have seen generational curses broken off in my family. I have seen demons being cast out. I have received financial breakthroughs. I have done an absolute fast for three days; on the third day, the Lord answered my prayer for a financial blessing. I received an unexpected blessing in an amount over four hundred dollars. Even after doing a fast for one day, I was able to receive an answer to a difficult decision I was facing.

Sometimes we make the decision to fast and decide what we will sacrifice. The reward comes when we follow through, but God sees our efforts. He rewards those who diligently seek him. We should always pray that our intentions during fasting and prayer are pure. We should not fast or pray with the intent to have harm done to others. God tells us to bless those who curse us and pray for those who spitefully use us. Allow the Lord to be your avenger.

There are different types of fasts. In a partial fast, certain foods are eliminated or you abstain from certain activities. I prefer fasting from foods. This is just my preference. Fasting is basically a sacrifice for God so that you may receive something in return. Sometimes a person may just fast to be more sensitive to the spirit of God.

Daniel fasted from meats, starches, and other foods. He only ate fruits and vegetables with water. Daniel declared that he would not eat the meat of the king, and he proved himself fairer than the rest of the king's men after ten days. If you are led to fast, I believe God will give you instructions on what fast to do. Sometimes we may belong to a church where leaders ask us to fast. This is a corporate fast and is very effective when a group is praying for the same results.

I have fasted many times and have also had my employees fast. I have a business, and my business is God-based. I do not force anyone to pray because it is a decision of the individual. However, I have discovered that God blesses us more when we come together. He blesses my business and my employees for their obedience. One thing that we should not do is replace sacrifice for obedience; the word says obedience is better than sacrifice.

Fasting along with praying has benefits for the mind, body, and soul. It helps keep your flesh under control. It destroys yokes in your life and in the lives of families and friends. My mom was once unsaved; after fasting and praying for forty days, God delivered her. The fast I did was a partial fast where I abstained from certain foods for a certain period of time. She now attends church regularly.

There is a lot of available information about fasting. You can search for scriptures and prayers for whatever you are fasting for. Make sure you are able to locate the information in the Bible. God is exceedingly abundant above all we ask or think.

The information in this chapter was brief, but I wanted to make sure the basics were covered. Realize that you gain wisdom when you fast and pray. Your decision making is clearer, and you receive answers speedily. You can read the following scriptures below for examples of fasts.

Absolute Fasts

Deuteronomy 9:9, 18
Ezra 10:6
Esther 4:16
Acts 9:9
Acts 27:33

Partial Fasts

1 Kings 17

Corporate Fasts

1 Samuel 7:5–6
2 Chronicles 20:3–4
Ezra 8:21–23
Nehemiah 9:1–13
Jonah 3:5–10

General Fasts

Isaiah 58:6–7
Daniel 1:8–16
Zachariah 7:5–10
Matthew 6:16–18
Luke 18:9–14
Jonah 3:8
1 Corinthians 7:5

CONCLUSION

Healing is an art and a science that requires education and knowledge of the word. "Study to shew thyself approved unto God, a workman that needeth not to be ashamed, rightly dividing the word of truth" (2 Timothy 2:15).

All problems have a solution, all diseases have a cure, and all brokenness can be made whole according to God's will and purpose for our lives. What God does not heal us from, or deliver us from, his grace is more than sufficient for us to live with it as conquerors—not as slaves!

We must pray, seek his face, change our wills, and transform our minds through the renewing of our minds. What we feed our minds is what our minds feed us. If we fill our minds with pleasurable things, positive words, and things of good report, our minds will give us pleasurable outcomes, positive endings, and rewards of good measure.